# Brevis Talk

*Wayne Whiteside*

"Brevis Talk," by Wayne Whiteside. ISBN 978-1-63868-180-9 (softcover); 978-1-63868-181-6 (Ebook).

Published 2024 by Virtualbookworm.com Publishing, P.O. Box 9949, College Station, TX 77842, US. ©2024, Mark Whiteside. All rights reserved. No part of this publication may be reproduced, stored in a retrieval system, or transmitted in any form or by any means, electronic, mechanical, recording or otherwise, without the prior written permission of Mark Whiteside.

*For my dear wife, Sheri, and our precious children, Christi and Tyler.*

# About the author

Wayne Whiteside's extensive experience in gospel ministry, spanning over 40 years, is a rich source of knowledge and insights. He has served as pastor of Crestview Baptist Church in Farmerville, Louisiana, for over 27 years. His travels to maximum security prison units (including death row) in 5 states further enrich his perspective.

# Preface

The following were taken from talks from the Brevis Talk Podcast. They have been edited in a few places from the original talks. It is my hope that these talks will speak to your heart in your journey with Christ.

A fellow traveler,
Wayne Whiteside

# Contents

About the author ..................................................................... iv

Preface ...................................................................................... v

The Quilt .................................................................................. 1

Jesus Is All I Need .................................................................. 4

Grace Precedes Truth ............................................................. 6

The Sound of Silence .............................................................. 8

Ole Scratch ............................................................................. 10

The Gospel Preacher ............................................................. 12

The Book That Blesses .......................................................... 15

Lessons From Some Vessels ................................................. 17

Vertical Vision ........................................................................ 19

Life Verses .............................................................................. 21

From Duty To Delight ........................................................... 22

Attitude Is Altitude ................................................................ 24

Hunting The Hunter .............................................................. 26

Muted Canines ....................................................................... 28

Air Preachers ......................................................................... 30

The Wonderment of God ...................................................... 32

Looking to Jesus .................................................................... 34

The 3rd Heaven ..................................................................... 36

The God of the Hills and Valleys ........................................ 38

Due Season ............................................................................. 40

The Perfect Pastor ................................................................. 41

Have You Become Unplugged? ........................................... 42

The Grieving Christian ................................................................. 44

Evidences of Revival ..................................................................... 46

Be Ready, Be Proclaiming, Be Kind ........................................... 48

From Within ................................................................................... 50

Lead me to the Rock ..................................................................... 52

The Wounded Traveler ................................................................. 54

Looking Forward ........................................................................... 56

God Leads His Dear Children ..................................................... 59

# The Quilt

## ...we are his workmanship...Ephesians 2:10

FOR EVERY BELIEVER IN JESUS CHRIST who's ever been knocked down, bloodied, and bruised by the circumstances of this life, there is a particular verse of Scripture that stands out. Romans chapter 8, verse 28 says "for God, causes all things to work together for good to those who love God and are called according to his purpose." That particular scripture has carried many a saint down through the ages.

I find myself going back to that scripture and it helps me to understand the puzzle and the questions of this life. You see this life is held ultimately in the hands of God. If something has been wrong in this life or something, if you've been wrong, God's going to make it right. One day, God's going to take care of everything. And he takes the good, the bad and the ugly circumstances of our lives and mixes them together. The sum total is good.

We are being made into the image of God. Dear one, you remember Joseph had problems. Abraham had problems. Moses had problems. You don't know anyone in the word of God who did not have problems. It's not always smooth sailing. This walk with God is not a Teflon road. It is full of bumps, curbs, twists, turns, broken glass, and barricades.

It is an obstacle course, so to speak, but God is with us. He will never leave us or forsake us. And in the end, everything we go through the sum total will add up to being good. Notice he talks about the called. This is not for everyone. This is for the called. I'm not going to get into some deep theological discussion here. I will simply say that the subject here is "the called." You know how I know I'm called? Because I answered when God called me to his salvation.

God called me to his son, Jesus Christ. And I answered the call. That makes me one of "the called." Someone might ask me if you've been called by God. Yes, I have been called. I remember the call and I answered the call. You don't know you're called until you've answered. And then this text says that we know, you know it helps a great deal to have this knowledge, even though our "why's" are not known here in this life, the old hymn writer said "we would understand it better by and by" what the scripture says that we can have faith in the fact that God is taking care of us and are in the hands of God.

Scripture says here, we know it is enough to know God. It is enough to know. God's plan is going to be realized and fulfilled in our lives. And then the text says that "all things work together for good." All things. The sum total in the end is good. Those things on the mountain that you experienced, those things in the valley, those things that are enjoyable, those things that are not so enjoyable, the happy times, the times of sorrow and pain, the times of fulfillment and the not so fulfilling times.

The sum total in the end is good. You might say good + ugly + sad = good. And you can add to the equation what you will, but the bottom line, the sum total is God mixes it together. God in his sovereignty and his power. And the ultimate sum total is G-O-O-D. Good. Now I want to tell you a little story.

My grandmother (she was actually my great grandmother) was a saint of God. She trusted in the Lord with her whole heart. My brother and I stayed at her home many times as children. And I especially remember that she always had a quilting project going on. She always had a quilt in her living room set up. And I remember as kids, we were real small, that quilt became a hiding place for hide and go seek.

We would get under that quilt. It was our fort, it was our tent, it was our teepee, and whatever our minds could imagine. Also,

I remember that someone would say what a beautiful quilt this is going to be; how it was turning out great. Well you know, as a little kid, I was under that quilt. There was no design. There was nothing beautiful about the backside of that quilt. I could see some thread hanging down. I could see some frayed knots here and there. And I never understood why people said that quilt was turning out so well.

And that it was so beautiful. I never understood that. But as I grew and got taller, I could to see the other side of that quilt. It was a beautiful thing to behold. It was beautiful. It was coming together.

My dear friend, we are not home yet. We're looking on the underside of God's handiwork. It makes no sense to us at this present moment. Perhaps all we can see at this moment is frayed knots. There doesn't seem to be a scheme, sketch, or pattern.

But when we get to the other side and we're able to look down at God's handiwork, we'll see the design, we'll see God's scheme and plan. And we will behold the beauty of his workmanship. We're not home yet. Consider the quilt. You and I are currently on the bottom side of this creation. But one day when God promotes us, we're going to be on the top side and it'll all fit together.

# Jesus Is All I Need

But seek ye first the kingdom of God, and his righteousness; and all these things shall be added unto you - Matthew 6:33

JESUS IS ALL I NEED
    Jesus is all I need
    I need no other friend
    I need no other one
    Jesus is all I need
    When I'm tired and I'm weary on my journey home
    When the road is rough and long and I feel so all alone
    When my strength is all gone and I can't carry on
    That's when my Jesus is all that I need.

**During a season of pain, sorrow, and loss -**

I was with a friend when he received word that his home was on fire. We rushed to the scene as the fire consumed all of his possessions. I will never forget the words that he spoke through tears in that moment, "The Lord gave, and the Lord has taken away; Blessed be the name of the Lord" (Job 1:21). This gentleman walked with God and these words were already planted within his heart.

Sometime soon after our son died, my wife and I talked and wondered what we were supposed to do? This is all we knew, "we've told others for years to lean on Jesus and He will be with you and give you strength and what you need. We've told others we are praying that the comfort of the Holy Spirit would be theirs in abundance. So, we are where many have been and now is no time to be a hypocrite. We will stand on the words that we've given to others." We are not strong people. But we do have a very strong and able Savior. And He is with us and was with us in the midst of the worst time in our lives.

In the evenings, we often sat silently in our recliners. We cried. We questioned. We got angry. In the background, we always had music playing. The artists, David Crowder and Rend Collective, will always be special to us. They became "close friends" as we walked through this terrible season in our lives. David Crowder's song, "All My Hope," has been and continues to be a wellspring in our lives.

**When you are tested or tried -**

1. It's not if, but when you are tested. You will be tested. You will go through trials in life.

2. This is the stuff that life is made of. Life is tough.

**David was an elderly man when he spoke these words -**

I have been young, and now am old; Yet I have not seen the righteous forsaken, Nor his descendants begging bread.  Psalm 37:25

**Other promises to consider during these seasons in life**

And my God will supply every need of yours according to his riches in glory in Christ Jesus.       Philippians 4:19

Peace I leave with you; my peace I give to you. Not as the world gives do I give to you. Let not your hearts be troubled, neither let them be afraid.  John 14:27

"Whom have I in heaven but you? I desire you more than anything on earth. My health may fail, and my spirit may grow weak, but God remains the strength of my heart; he is mine forever." ~ Psalm 73:25-26

**The sufficiency of Jesus -**

There are companions who harm one another, but there is a friend who sticks closer than a brother. Proverbs 18:24

"You may never know that Jesus is all you need, until Jesus is all you have." - Corrie Ten Boom

# Grace Precedes Truth

## grace and truth came by Jesus Christ - John 1:17

THE WORD "GRACE" comes before the word "truth" in these 2 verses (John 1:14,17)

My personal opinion is that the Bible was written and preserved as God intended it to be. It is the inspired Word of God. We are called to "grace" people and then an opportunity to speak the truth will perhaps come. Some would call this relational ministry.

We see the tenderness of Jesus in his conversation with the woman caught in adultery(John 8:1-11), the Rich Young Ruler (Luke 18:18-23), and the woman at the well (John 4:4-30). He connected with these individuals, then spoke truth to them.

Grace people, be kind, be merciful. Hear their story. Listen to them. This is the outline and order in which ministry takes place.

We are called to be ambassadors, reconcilers, and heralds of the gospel message. Our kind and merciful demeanor to and before all is part of the calling of God upon our lives.

I must confess that I don't always get this right; I'm a falling, fumbling follower of Jesus Christ. But in the innermost place of my heart, I want to get this right.

I remember many years ago meeting and visiting with a young man named John who was an inmate in a maximum security unit. I spoke briefly with John as I was walking from cell to cell and speaking with the men in that facility. I asked John if he had any prayer requests? He replied, "yes, please pray for my children, John Junior and Susie."

Six weeks later, I was back at the prison unit. I walked up to John's cell greeting him and I asked about his children, John Junior and Susie." His response was, "you remembered their names!"

I said, "Yes, John, I've been praying for them." If there was any obstacle or wall between us, then it fell that day. From that time forward, we talked across a number of subjects. Somewhere down the road I was able to share the hope and love of Jesus Christ to John. He later became a believer and faithful follower of our Lord.

Grace opens the door to truth.

# The Sound of Silence

But the Lord is in his holy temple: let all the earth keep silence before him - Habakkuk 2:20

THERE'S A QUIETNESS OF THE SOUL for Habakkuk and he's not happy about it. He complains to God, as is recorded in the first chapter, verse 2, "O Lord, how long shall I cry, and You will not hear?..."

I know individuals that once they have gotten home will turn on their televisions or play music simply because they don't like the sound of nothing. Silence.

They have perhaps an insecurity in the presence of silence.

God was silent and Habakkuk interpreted this as God not being active and working. He could not have been more incorrect.

So, what we have are a series of complaints that Habakkuk levels at God in a very accusatory voice. And then God replies. The first thing that God says is that the injustice in the land will be dealt with. He tells Habakkuk that he is raising up a fierce group of people to invade the land and punish the disobedient severely. He goes on to describe these people and the harsh manner in which they will deal with the current leaders.

Then, Habakkuk complains that these invaders are even worse than the people of God. We are not unlike Habakkuk in that we want God to deal with the problem, but then we complain when God deals with the problem.

It's like when we pray "God use me" and then someone is difficult and we complain "I'm being used." We want to be used by God, but not to be uncomfortable.

## Hush Habakkuk

In chapter 2, verse 20 that's essentially what God told the prophet. Be quiet before Me. I'm in my temple. I am in control. Be quiet and you will discern this.

Shoosh, people of God. God is active and involved in the affairs of humanity. God's wheels of justice grind slowly, but they grind surely. Just because you can't see movement, it doesn't mean that God is not at work.

# Ole Scratch

### ...pray always...Luke 21:36

ARE YOU IN SUCH A SITUATION that you feel parlayzed? Do you feel that you are unlearned, insufficient, and ungifted in the area of prayer? Yet, the circumstances of life bid you to pray. You must pray, for situations in life demand it and without God's intervention we are utterly defeated.

Be encouraged from the Scriptures! We are called and summoned to pray "...according to the power that works in us (Ephesians 3:20).

Within the child of God resides the Comforter, the Helper, the Teacher, the Intercessor...the Holy Spirit.

Likewise the Spirit also helps us in our weakness: for we know not what we should pray for as we ought: but the Spirit himself makes intercession for us with groanings which cannot be uttered (Romans 8:26).

**We are told to pray -**

Pray without ceasing (1 Thessalonians 5:17).

Pray for one another...Confess your faults one to another, and pray one for another, that ye may be healed. The effectual fervent prayer of a righteous man availeth much (James 5:16)

**Things happen when we pray -**

A repentant thief who died next to Jesus made a petition and it changed his destiny(Luke 22:40-43).

Transfiguration of Christ - (Luke 9:28).

Outpouring of the Holy Spirit was during a prayer meeting - (Acts 2).

Deliverance of Peter from prison and a certain death the next day - (Acts 12:13).

Two dogs met every morning in their neighborhood. These two dogs could not be more unlike than the other. One was a small terrier who lived indoors with his family. His name was Scratch. The other canine was a large outdoor dog named Tank.

During the mornings they met up enjoying each other's companionship. One particular morning as it was getting hot, Scratch said, "I'm going to go back inside." Tank asked him, "How do you get back inside?"

Scratch paused and replied to Tank, "I really don't understand it. All I know is that when I scratch the door, it opens."

Luke 11:9 tells us, "knock(or in this case scratch) and it will be opened to you.

# The Gospel Preacher

...they ceased not to teach and preach Jesus Christ - Acts 5:42

MOREOVER, BRETHREN, I DECLARE UNTO YOU the gospel which I preached unto you, which also you have received, and in which you stand; 2 By which also you are saved, if you keep in memory what I preached unto you, unless you have believed in vain. 3 For I delivered unto you first of all that which I also received, how that Christ died for our sins according to the scriptures; 4 And that he was buried, and that he rose again the third day according to the scriptures (1 Corinthians 15:1-4).

**The gospel preacher**

I'm being specific because the message is specific. It may be out of fashion or perhaps the current wind that is blowing in the church world, but I will use the term "gospel preacher" intentionally. He's not just a speaker, a lecturer, a sermonizer, reverend, clergy, minister, or pastor and I certainly hope he speaks with more authority than to be called "someone who is on our staff."

He can be all of these titles and not a gospel preacher. We need more gospel preachers. Perhaps some in ministry should do some fresh inventory about their calling and ask themselves, "am I a gospel preacher?" And let me say, that no, I don't have some special insight that no one else has. I'm a simple sinner, saved by the blood of Jesus Christ, who has been called into ministry. In the many years since I was called I've had to refocus, reexamine, and repent often. I do hope and pray that as I step toward the sunset of my life that I can say with the apostle Paul, "For I am determined not to know anything among you except Jesus Christ and Him crucified" (1 Corinthians 2:2).

So, let's jump in, by first of all, defining the gospel message -

**1. Definition of the gospel message.**

    A. Proclamation of good news.

        1. The gospel is good news in a fallen world.

        2. Good news shines bright against the dark background of our world and culture.

    B. Proclamation of a Person.

        1. Gospel is a person. He is wonderful and His name is Jesus.

        2. The gospel is not an act, like christening, baptism, partaking of communion, church attendance, etc. God's only begotten Son, Christ Jesus, the Lord and Savior, is the gospel.

    C. Proclamation of that Person's activities.

        1. His death.

        2. His burial.

        3. His resurrection.

**2. Demeanor of the gospel preacher.**

    A. He is blessed and privileged to speak " the unsearchable riches of Christ" (Ephesians 3:8).

    B. He is weak - "Therefore I take pleasure in infirmities, in reproaches, in necessities, in persecutions, in distresses for Christ's sake: for when I am weak, then am I strong" (2 Corinthians 12:10).

    C. His badge is love - "As the Father hath loved me, so have I loved you: continue ye in my love" (John 15:9).

**3. Decisional preaching.**

Spurgeon said that no matter what he preached about, toward the conclusion of the message, he made a beeline to the cross.

    A. Every sermon from a gospel preacher should have a similar ending.

B. He exhorts and desires to stir people to see that time is short in this life and eternity is closer than we think.

C. Come to Jesus is the call. He will forgive you of your sins. He will save you.

May God raise up more gospel preachers in these last days!

# The Book That Blesses

I will delight myself in thy statutes: I will not forget thy word - Psalm 119:16

THE PSALMIST SAYS IN A COUPLE OF PLACES that "our delight is in the law of the Lord. And in the law we are to meditate day and night." The psalmist says in another place, "I will delight myself in your statutes. I will not forget your word."

Someone has said concerning the Bible that the book is the mind of God. The state of man, the way of salvation, the doom of sinners and the happiness of believers.

It's doctrines are holy, it's precepts convicts, its histories are true and its decisions are immutable.

Read it to be wise. Believe it to be safe, practice it to be holy.

It contains light to direct you. Food, to sustain you and comfort to cheer you. It is the Traveler's map, the Pilgrim's staff, the pilot's compass, the soldier's sword and the Christian's character.

Here paradise is restored. Heaven is opened. And the gates of hell disclosed. Christ is its grand subject. Our good, its design and the glory of God, its end.

It should fill the memory, rule the heart and move the feet. Read it slowly, frequently, and prayerfully. It is a mine of wealth, a paradise of glory and a river of pleasure.

Follow its precepts, and it will lead you to Calvary, to the empty tomb, and to a resurrected life in Christ. Yes, to glory itself for eternity.

The blessed book that blesses.

# Lessons From Some Vessels

...they ceased not to teach and preach Jesus Christ - 2 Corinthians 4:7

MANY YEARS AGO I REMEMBER the story of a gentleman getting very upset at a friend of his who attended the same church with him.

It seems that a very well known quartet group came to the church on a Sunday evening and put on a concert. The man who was upset had missed the concert and wanted to know why his friend had not told him that they were coming.

His friend told him that if he was even a nominal attender of the church services that he would know. He told him that the group's concert had been announced for several Sundays.

This silenced the man who was upset.

Sometimes blessings come to those who just show up.

I want to speak with you for a few moments about vessels of honor(blessing):

Therefore if anyone cleanses himself from the latter, he will be a vessel for honor, sanctified and useful for the Master, prepared for every good work.

2 Timothy 2:21

There's a story hidden deeply in the Old Testament(where some Christians hardly ever visit) in 2 Kings and it goes like this: One day the widow of a member of the group of prophets came to Elisha and cried out, "My husband who served you is dead, and you know how he feared the Lord. But now a creditor has come, threatening to take my two sons as slaves." "What can I do to help you?" Elisha asked. "Tell me, what do you have in the house?"

"Nothing at all, except a jar of oil," she replied. And Elisha said, "Borrow as many empty jars as you can from your friends and neighbors. Then go into your house with your sons and shut the door behind you. Pour oil from your flask into the jars, setting each one aside when it is filled."

So she did as she was told. Her sons kept bringing jars to her, and she filled one after another. 6 Soon every container was full to the brim! "Bring me another jar," she said to one of her sons. "There aren't any more!" he told her. And then the oil stopped flowing.

2 Kings 4:1-6

These vessels were:

**Empty** - Can't fill full vessels. Many of us are so full of the world and it's offerings, that there is no room to be filled by God. We must do some soul cleaning and emptying.

Make room for the things of God. Throw some things out.

**Open** - Can't fill a vessel with a lid on the top of it. Many aren't and will never be filled because they like the status quo and are not open to God and His truth. You don't know all the truth and you certainly aren't walking in all of the truth, so get over yourself. Pride keeps us from being open to God. Pride says I know and I have arrived.

**Available** - Something amazingly simple about just being present; showing up.

**Upright** - can't pour horizontally into a vessel. We must be upright if God is to pour into our lives. Don't diminish this necessary position of upright living.

What kind of vessel are you? One of honor or dishonor?

# Vertical Vision

...look to the rock from which you were cut...Isaiah 51:1

1 Samuel 17
AND THE PHILISTINE(Goliath) drew near morning and evening, and presented himself forty days. For 40 days, twice a day, Goliath taunted the army of Israel. That's 80 viewings.

The movie Goliath was played over and over. And who knows how often they had rewound the tape and replayed it in their minds? This mountain of a warrior struck fear in the hearts of the Hebrew soldiers. The vision and perhaps the shadow, was cast upon their faces and seared within their minds.

**Same scene - two different viewings.**

A horizontal view states that Goliath is big. A vertical view says God is bigger than Goliath.

A horizontal view says that Goliath is too large to defeat. A vertical view tells us that Goliath is too big to miss as a target.

The Hebrew army's view was horizontal and they could not see vertically. David, the young shepherd boy, arrives on the scene and his view is vertical. His view during the journey to check on his brothers has been the expanse of the sky and the stars. He sees upward and comprehends that humans are like grasshoppers before their Creator. Goliath is indeed small when put in perspective against the handiwork of God.

There's a world of difference in how they were seeing things.

A man was driving in the country one day and he saw an old man sitting on a fence rail watching the cars go by. Stopping to pass the time of day, the traveler said, "I never could stand living out here. You don't see anything, and I'm sure you don't travel like I do. I'm on the go all the time."

The old man on the fence looked down at the stranger and drawled, "I can't see much difference in what I'm doing and what you're doing. I sit on the fence and watch the autos go by and you sit in your auto and watch the fences go by. It's just the way you look at things."

We are admonished in Colossians 3:2, "to set your minds on the things above, not the things on earth."

# Life Verses

## All scripture is given by inspiration of God...2 Timothy 3:16

IN NO WAY AM I SUGGESTING that one portion or verse of Scripture is more important than any other. I am saying that there are verses of Scripture that perhaps have especially echoed within your soul and continue to do so. I call them life verses because they spoke to you and continue to speak to you on your journey. Here are a few of mine:

Psalm 46:1 - *God is our refuge and strength, a* **VERY PRESENT HELP** *in trouble.*

John 3:30 - ***He** must **increase**, but **I** must **decrease**.*

John 14:6 - *Jesus saith unto him,* <u>*I am the way*</u>*,* <u>*the truth*</u>*, and* <u>*the life*</u>*: no man comes to the Father, but by me.*

Philippians 4:13 - *I can do all things through Christ which strengthens me.*

The words are the same, just rearranged. The new arrangement helps me see this truth in a fresh way:

Through Christ who gives me strength...I can do all things.

What are your life verses?

# From Duty To Delight

I delight to do your will, O my God: yes, your law is within my heart - Psalm 40:8

I ONCE HEARD SOMEONE SAY that "they had to sing" at the church next week. I thought to myself, "No. you get to sing" at the church next week.

That got me thinking about the two types of people who are serving the Lord: Those out of a sense of duty and those who are serving because they are delighted by the Lord and the privilege of serving Him.

I want to take a few moments of your time and speak about the subject:

...from duty to delight

Duty is good and honorable.

Duty is noble. Duty will accomplish many things.

Duty to the Lord, family, country, an occupation.

Duty will finish the task.

But there's an even **higher call** in the Christian journey. It is to move from duty to delight.

Some never move from duty to delight.

It is the will of God that we serve Him out of a heart of joy and gratitude, rather than being just someone who completes the task.

Do you hear the word "attitude" in "gratitude?" It's there.

I think duty has its eye on the task and delight has its eye on the Lord.

There was this man who simply wanted to enjoy a Sunday afternoon nap. Next to his home was a vacant lot where the local kids in the neighborhood would gather and play baseball. They were loud and numerous times this man would ask them to be a little quieter, to no avail.

So, after thinking through the problem, he came up with a plan. The next Sunday afternoon he spoke to the kids and said, "I'll pay you each a dollar for playing baseball." The kids were confused at his change of heart toward their baseball games, but asked "are you serious? You will pay us to play baseball?" He said, "beginning next Sunday, I will pay you."

They gathered, they played, and he paid. They gathered a few more weeks, the same result - they played and he paid. After a few weeks, he told the boys, "I'm going to give you all a raise. I will pay you $2 for each game you play." They couldn't believe what they were hearing, but quickly agreed. This went on for a few weeks and the man broke the news to them that he would no longer be able to pay them. The boys complained and pleaded with the man to continue paying them. Exasperated, they agreed as a group not to play anymore if the man wouldn't pay them.

The man got his nap, because the boys got their eyes off of the delight of simply playing baseball.

There's a higher calling than just serving the Lord out of duty. From duty to delight. That's stepping upward.

# Attitude Is Altitude

Let this mind be in you, which was also in Christ Jesus - Philippians 2:5

**Word association -**
Bee, hive, honey
Delicious, dessert, chocolate

**Attitude** - mental state
**Altitude** - a distance measurement in the vertical direction
Some words from the hymn, Higher Ground:
...new heights I'm gaining every day...

More word association -
attitude and gratitude
A truly great discipline and practice comes from a hymn writer:
Count your blessings, name them one by one,
Count your blessings, see what God has done!

**Attitude**
by Charles Swindoll
"THE LONGER I LIVE, the more I realize the impact of attitude on life. Attitude, to me, is more important than facts.

It is more important than the past, than education, than money, than circumstances, than failures, than successes, than what other people think or say or do.

It is more important than appearance, giftedness, or skill.

It will make or break a company ... a church ... a home.

The remarkable thing is we have a choice every day regarding the attitude we will embrace for that day.

We cannot change the inevitable.

The only thing we can do is play on the one string we have, and that is our attitude ...

I am convinced that life is 10% what happens to me, and 90% how I react to it.

And so it is with you ... we are in charge of our Attitudes."

# Hunting The Hunter

## For the Son of man is come to seek and to save that which was lost - Luke 19:10

The "Most Dangerous Game" by Richard Connell is a story about Sanger Rainsford, one of the world's most celebrated big game hunters. Rainsford has a boating accident while enroute to a hunting expedition along the coast of South America. He manages to swim safely to an island. On the island he finds a castle. This castle is inhabited by a Russian nobleman, named General Zaroff. He, too, is a big game hunter and during their conversation he proceeds to tell Rainsford that he is hunting a "new animal" on the island.

As their conversation continues, Rainsford comes to realize that General Zaroff intends to hunt him. The hunter has become the hunted.

On a much higher level, that is what the Book of Acts, chapter 9, is about; the pursuer becomes the pursued.

Saul, the persecutor of the church and pursuer of believers becomes the hunted as God pursues him.

**God has a plan.**

Never write anyone off. This self righteous man was "breathing out threats and murder" we are told in verse 1.

I missed it big time a few years back. There was a man who was wonderfully converted. I didn't say this out loud, but in my heart *'I thought if ever there was a man who is not going to come to Christ, then it's this man.'* I'm happy to report today that I was very wrong. He did come to Christ and after many years continues to walk with Jesus and is a mighty witness of God's power to change someone.

**God pursues man for good.**

His desire and intention is to save them from their sins and give them not only eternal life, but an abundant life now.

...the goodness of God leads you to repentance - Rom 2:4

All things work together for good... - Rom 8:28

**God changes us.**

You cannot have an encounter with Jesus and be the same you.

That's just not possible. I'm not speaking here of sinless perfection in this life, but rather salvation and continuous sanctification as we travel this journey of Christian living.

So the storyline in Acts chapter 9 is that God hunted the hunter(Paul), and captured him.

# Muted Canines

His watchmen are blind, All of them know nothing. All of them are mute dogs unable to bark... - Isaiah 56:10

*For there are certain men crept in unawares, who were before of old ordained to this condemnation, ungodly men, turning the grace of our God into lasciviousness, and denying the only Lord God, and our Lord Jesus Christ*

Jude 1:4

IN THE NOT TOO DISTANT PAST, most homes in the rural South had a familiar tenant. He was usually an outside resident, but not always. He was as small as perhaps 10 lbs or would weigh over 100 lbs. He was an "alarmist" by nature and by heart. He might be a mongrel or a purebreed, but his worth was being on "watch," hence his utilitarian title, "watchdog."

He seems to have almost disappeared from the current landscape. That's not the only location the "watchdog" is often missing.

The New Testament pastor fulfilled the role of "watchdog," sounding the alarm to his flock. The congregation was warned about worldliness and belief systems that were contrary to Scripture's teachings.

There are still "watchdogs" within the body of Christ. However, they are not as plentiful as in previous days.

*Many of today's pulpit inhabitants fulfill the words of Isaiah, "...they are mute dogs, they cannot bark..."* (Isaiah 56:10)

The called of God knows that often a "thus saith the Lord" message conflicts with popularity, and the blowing winds of faddish living.

Although this is not exhaustive, in a brief talk as this, I can think of 3 words that are perhaps extinct from some American pulpits; sin, hell, and repentance.

Paul tells Timothy that "the time will come when they will not endure sound doctrine, but according to their own desires, because they have itching ears, they will heap up for themselves teachers." (2 Timothy 4:3)

Only eternity will reveal how many false teachings "have crept in unnoticed" (Jude 1:4) because the "watchdogs" cannot or will not bark.

Thank God for the watchdogs that seek to guard the flock of God.

# Air Preachers

How long shall this be in the heart of the prophets that prophesy lies? yea, they are prophets of the deceit of their own heart - Jeremiah 23:26

HERE IS A PUFFED UP TITLE for some puffed up people - Pitiful Piddling Peddler Prophets Propagating Prevarications

False prophets are no prophets. Jeremiah was speaking for God when he said **"they prophesy lies in My name"**. (Jeremiah 14:14; 23:25, 26, 32) These were men of no substance. Pure fluff. The wind of their many words. No authority. No anointing. Windy emptiness.

**Peddlers**

**Motivation**- deceitful hearts (Jer 23:26)
1. Popularity
2. Attention seekers - "me,me, and more me" syndrome
3. A daughter said this about her dad(a former president) - My father always wanted to be the corpse at every funeral, the bride at every wedding, and the baby at every christening. (Alice Roosevelt)
4. Financial gain - *For we are not, as so many, peddling the word of God...*2 Corinthians 2:17

Then, there are the real(sincere servants) of God.
1. They speak the truth from God's Word.
2. They speak from a heart that has love for the Lord and as a result they desire to please God rather than man.

I, therefore, the prisoner of the Lord, beseech you to walk worthy of the calling with which you were called - Ephesians 4:1

**Worthy - axios** (Greek)
1. Weigh in, drawing down the scale.
2. Substance.

Outer appearances are often just that; outer appearances.

Look at the difference between a rice cake and a dollar coin.
1. The rice cake is much larger in size than the dollar coin.
2. But when you think of substance and durability, the winner is clearly the dollar coin.
3. And here's the bigger contrast, while the rice cake is larger its weight is 3 grams, while the dollar coin weight 8.1 grams.

On the scales of God, the air preacher doesn't move them, he's a lightweight in every way imaginable.

The preacher who walks worthy of the Lord preaches a message of substance from a heart of substance.

# The Wonderment of God

The heavens declare the glory of God and the expanse proclaims the work of His hands - Psalm 19:11

HAVE YOU LOST THE WONDERMENT or that state of being in awe of God? I know that it is popular to say the word "awesome" today about any and everything, but that really is a word that should have God's copyright.
**God is awesome.**

A recent study showed that there is a definite correlation between those who are in outside of buildings and enclosures and mental health. Their suggestion? To the government - build more parks. To the people - get outside.

Our Lord told us in Matthew 18:3, to become as children.

I believe that children can teach us a great deal about the "wonderment of God"(state of wonder).

Or if you need a refresher course, hang out with some little people and let them teach you and remind you about the bigness and nearness of God and the beauty of His creation.

Some time ago, my granddaughter and I were outside. She came across a beautiful little flower. She said over and over how pretty it was. And she looked at me and asked me if I knew who made that flower? I said, "God made it." With a big smile on her face, she replied, "Yes, He makes all of the flowers."

Get outside and listen and see as the "heavens declare the glory of God…"

A friend was telling me of a little boy in his community that after seeing a centipede for the first time, said, "He's got a lot of fingerprints."

The wonder of it all. Dear friend, let me say it one more time - Get outside!

# Looking to Jesus

## looking unto Jesus... Hebrews 12:2

A. Encouragement from the past.
   1. Are you weary? Tired? Troubled? Persecuted? Paralyzed by fear? Look to Jesus.
   2. Read chapter 11 of Hebrews. It is a rich narrative of those who have gone before us(the cloud of witnesses) as they have walked with God, endured much and now have safely arrived to their eternal home. In this chapter, you will find that they hid in caves, were sawn into, imprisoned, executed, etc. Your current pain and challenges have been experienced by those who have gone before you. Do as they have done - look to Jesus. Don't give Jesus your best. Give Him your all. Be "all in" with Him and His kingdom. When Jesus went to the Cross, He was "all in" for you.

B. Exhortation to complete the race.

A preacher friend who has been a large person all of his life was telling me about what sports he was involved in while in high school. He told me about his experiences playing football, basket ball, and track.

I asked him, "Track? Did you throw the shot put?"
He said, "No."
I asked, "Discus thrower?"
He said, "No. I ran long distance."
I said, "What did you say? Running?"

He said, "Yep, I was a long distance runner."

I asked, "How so?"

He replied, "I won races, because I decided I ain't quitting. And I never quit a race. I lost some, but I won some, too."

**Endurance = I ain't quitting.**

Hebrews 12:1 - Lay aside some things - **there are some things that you are holding onto.**

The sin that easily ensnares - **there is something that is holding onto you.**

**C. Eyes upon Jesus.**
1. I wish I had the ability to jolt every Christian to this statement, LOOK TO JESUS.
2. You don't need some magical, mystical experience.
3. The next book you read is not going to change your life.
4. You need to chase after the Son of God. Pursue Jesus. Hunger after Him. Thirst after Him.
5. Get your gaze off of this world and this life. It is passing away.

Turn your eyes upon Jesus
Look full, in his wonderful face
And the things of earth will grow strangely dim
In the light of his glory and grace.

# The 3rd Heaven

I know a man in Christ who fourteen years ago was caught up to the third heaven. Whether it was in the body or out of the body I do not know—God knows. 2 Corinthians 12:2

WE SHOULD NOT ALLOW THE MYSTICS or charlatans to "explain" this verse of Scripture. Let us take a forthright approach in our understanding.

The Word used for "heaven" in the New Testament is a very generalized term. It can be interpreted as "air, sky, the place of the sun, moon, stars or God's dwelling place."

**Hence, the "first" heaven is understood to be the air or sky -**
But the land that you are going over to possess is a land of hills and valleys, which drinks water by the rain from heaven
(Deuteronomy 11:11).

**The "second" heaven where the stars and planets reside -**
When I look at your heavens, the work of your fingers,
the moon and the stars, which you have set in place
(Psalm 8:3).

**The "third" heaven is the dwelling place of God -**
Our Father in heaven,
hallowed be your name (Matthew 6:9).

**From our current location, consider this statement:**

We see the first heaven by day, the second heaven by night, and the third heaven by faith.

# The God of the Hills and Valleys

...you shall know that I am the Lord(1 King 20:28).

THEN THE SERVANTS OF THE KING OF SYRIA said to him, "Their gods *are* gods of the hills. Therefore they were stronger than we; but if we fight against them in the plain, surely we will be stronger than they.

Then a man of God came and spoke to the king of Israel, and said, "Thus says the Lord: 'Because the Syrians have said, "The Lord *is* God of the hills, but He *is* not God of the valleys," therefore I will deliver all this great multitude into your hand, and you shall know that I *am* the Lord.' (1 Kings 20:23, 28).

**The Syrians were limiting God** - countless people limit God; the Spirit filled believer puts no handcuffs on a Holy God. He's God Almighty. He can and will do as He pleases. Nothing is impossible with God.

In the last days, there will be a people who have a form of godliness but **deny God's power** (2 Timothy 3:5).
  1. Their "form" of Godliness defines God by their own standard, rather than the fruits of the Spirit.
  2. They deny His power. Perhaps, they "interpret" God according to a time period or dispensation? They might say, "He doesn't do/work like that anymore." The truth is that He's God and He will do what He pleases to do(Psalm 115:3).

3. Those unexplainable truths that are above us and must be taken by faith; virgin birth, resurrection, a triune God.

**Horizontal vision?**

1. The psalmist stated "I will lift up my eyes to the hills—From whence comes my help? My help *comes* from the Lord, Who made heaven and earth" (Psalm 121:1-2).
2. If then you were raised with Christ, seek those things which are above, where Christ is, sitting at the right hand of God. Set your mind on things above, not on things on the earth (Colossians 3:1-2).

The valleys and the mountains do not dictate or limit God's ability. He created them and He holds all of creation in the hollow of His hand. His ability is limitless. His plan will not be thwarted. He is God above and beyond any circumstances.

# Due Season

### ...we shall reap...Galatians 6:9

AND LET US NOT GROW WEARY while doing good, for in due season we shall reap if we do not lose heart.   Galatians 6:9

"Due season" can be interpreted as "the assigned time." We will reap a harvest of good from the Father.

What's the requirement from us? Do not quit, do not abandon the work of the King. When we "grow weary," we become disheartened and we stop.

So press on(soldier on). Although perhaps tired and bruised, we're almost home.

The sunset of time is near. Be found in the field working for Jesus. Don't "lose heart" and stop. The Father rewards those who labor for Him.

O land of rest, for thee I sigh! When will the moment come When I shall lay my armor by And dwell in peace at home?

We'll work till Jesus comes, We'll work till Jesus comes, We'll work till Jesus comes, And we'll be gathered home.

# The Perfect Pastor

1. The perfect pastor's been found. He is able to make everyone happy and happy at the same time.

2. He preaches exactly 15 minutes and then sits down.

3. He condemns sin, but never makes anyone feel uncomfortable.

4. He works from 8 in the morning to 10 at night, doing everything from preaching sermons to sweeping.

5. He makes $400 per week, gives $300 a week to the church, drives a car that's not new, but it's not too old, either.

6. He is tall on the short side, heavy-set in a thin sort of way, and handsome.

7. He eyes are blue or brown, (to fit the occasion) and wears his hair parted in the middle - left side, dark and straight, right side, brown and wavy.

8. He has a burning desire to work with the youth, and spends all his time with the senior citizens.

9. He smiles all the time while keeping a straight face, because he has a keen sense of humor that finds him seriously dedicated.

12. He makes 15 calls a day on church members, spends all his time evangelizing non-members, and is always found in his study if he is needed.

Unfortunately, he died at 32 years of age.

# Have You Become Unplugged?

HERE'S A LIGHTHEARTED STORY and some applications: Many years ago at our church on a particular day, there was just a lot of activity going on at the same time. I think there was a serviceman or two doing some maintenance, someone delivering packages, and a dear saint who was vacuuming the back hallway. The back hallway is a very long pathway. He had begun vacuuming around the corner from the hallway and made his way into the hallway. Now, this gentleman has a hearing deficiency. He was pushing this upright vacuum cleaner back and forth with great effort. (Please know that this gentleman and I are good friends) Well, I unplugged the vacuum cleaner and because of the perfect storm of activity and his hearing deficiency, he wasn't aware that it was unplugged. So, back and forth, he pushes and pushes the vacuum cleaner. After a few moments, he does notice that the vacuum cleaner is not picking up things as well as it was. So, what does he do? He pushes the vacuum cleaner faster and faster across the carpet. After a bit, he stops and he's breathing hard. He looks down the hallway and sees me laughing. Longer story made short, we both have a good laugh about it all.

Now, here's an observation or two maybe toward our Christian walk and the Holy Spirit. The Holy Spirit is the source of our power and strength for all things in our spiritual journey.

The 1st observation is:
1. He wasn't aware that he had become unplugged.
2. He exerted himself more and more and produced the same results.

**Have you come unplugged?**
1. 1.Keep an eye on the outlet.
2. Don't presume that because you were once plugged in that you continue to be.

**Things can pull us away**
1. Distractions(wandering); the busyness of life.
2. Sins will separate us from the power source; the Holy Spirit.
3. The noise, because of all the activity around, kept my friend from hearing the humming of the vacuum cleaner.

# The Grieving Christian

*But I do not want you to be ignorant, brethren, concerning those who have fallen asleep, lest you sorrow as others who have no hope.*

1 Thess 4:13

DECEMBER THE 14TH is always a difficult day for me and my family. It was on this day that our dear son, Tyler, went home to be with the Lord. We grieve and we will grieve over his death until the end of our days. But we do not grieve as many grieve.

Our grief is a grief which has much hope and confidence. The text that I read at the beginning of this podcast speaks of those who grieve with no hope. That is the tragedy of tragedies.

Let me share a few thoughts about dying and the Christian. First of all, numerous times in the New Testament we see death being described as falling asleep. For a Christian to die is to fall asleep in this life and to awaken in the Presence of Jesus and all of the brothers and sisters in Christ who preceded us in death.

The Greek word used for death here is asleep or "to lie down." The same word which would later become the word "cemetery," meaning a "sleeping place."

Let me use 3 marks of punctuation to illustrate death and the believer in Christ. First, a period speaks of a certain finality. But death is not the end of life for the believer.

And a question mark would be highly inaccurate to use because there is no question about where the departed in Jesus resides. Second Corinthians chapter 5 tells us that to be absent from the body is to be present with the Lord. We have a know-so faith. First John chapter 5 says that these things have been written so you know that you have eternal life. (1 John 5:13) The preceding verses tell us that this life is in God's Son, Jesus.

So, what punctuation mark would I deem as most accurate in defining death and the Christian? Well, that would be the comma. For you see, a comma denotes that there is a pause, but then a continuation picks up afterward. To die in this life in Jesus is but a momentary pause. And so when we attend a funeral for a departed brother or sister in Christ it is certainly not to say goodbye, but rather "I'll see you later."

And, so, because of Jesus, my heart says concerning my son, "I'll see you soon, Tyler."

# Evidences of Revival

THE EVIDENCE OF A REVIVAL IS DISPLAYED in Nehemiah 8:1-10. The Hebrew children displayed evidences of true revival at the completion of the wall. And Christians can display evidences of true revival. Let's glean some truths from this passage.

First of all, we see **harmony among the people**. Verse. One says that the people gathered as one. We see the power of the early church in the first century and the book of acts that narrative collection and the Bible says they were in one accord. We often see in that narrative that they were unified. There is power in one. God is grieved when his children have dissension among them, God is grieved when there are ill feelings toward one another. Unity and the power of one accord are evidence of revival.

Secondly, there's a **hunger for the word** chapter eight, again, verse three, all the people were attentive to the book of the law, a hunger, an attention grabbing hunger for the word of God.

They were attentive. They listened to the word of God. The writer of the book of Hebrew says in chapter five, I've got a lot to tell you, Hebrews, but you are dull of hearing. The Bible says in the book of Revelation, he, that has an ear, let him hear. And so there's something to be said about Spirit filled listening, a hunger for the word, and then honor for the Lord. Verse six tells us they bowed low and worshiped the Lord. They honored God's name. They honored the remembrance of God. There was a certain humility there for the Lord. They bowed low and they worshiped the Lord. The greatest among you will be the servant. It's not that way in the world. It's a rush to the top, but Jesus turned the world upside down. He said, the first will be last. And the last will be first.

Verse 9 - **Heartfelt repentance** – All the people were weeping when they heard the Word of God. The Word is convicting. It is a two-edged sword. You know, it'd be wonderful and refreshing if some shame were to be seen in our world today. There seems to be little shame today. Many years ago, they perhaps would be ashamed. What was once shameful behavior is paraded on our streets today. There is no shame in our culture. Even more troubling oftentimes there is no shame among the so-called people of God.

And then we see a **happiness in the Lord**. Verse 10 says for the joy of the Lord is your strength.

Oh, I'm around too many people who name the name of Christ that are like sticks in the mud. They are joyless. Christianity for them is like stomach problems to be endured. Joyless. Absolutely without a certain joy of the Lord.

You know, children were attracted to Jesus Christ and I don't believe he walked around with a frown and a grimace on his face. Children would not be drawn to such a person. I believe Jesus walked with joy in his heart. The Bible says He ran the race for the joy that was set before him.(Hebrews 12:2) There's a certain happiness in the Lord that we can have in our journey.

# Be Ready, Be Proclaiming, Be Kind

**BE SAVED.**

2 Corinthians 6:2 - behold, now is the accepted time; behold, now is the day of salvation.

Romans 10:13 - Whoever calls on the name of the Lord will be saved.

**BE READY:** An admonition from the Bible.

Mt 24:44; Luke 12:40 - Therefore you also be ready, for the Son of Man is coming at an hour you do not expect.

Are you ready? You can be ready. Call on Jesus to deliver you from your sins; to forgive you.

**BE PROCLAIMING.**

2 Timothy 4:2 - Preach the word! Be ready in season *and* out of season. Convince, rebuke, exhort, with all longsuffering and teaching.

1. Preach - to proclaim openly, herald
2. Newspaper hawkers - "Extra! Extra! Read all about it…"
3. To everyone. It's like fishing. Not every fish will bite, but if you don't cast(proclaim), you will never catch a fish.
4. Know how to witness. Be intentional in learning. There several good ways. You could learn and possibly memorize what is called the Romans Road(Romans 3:23; 6:23; 10:9,13). Evangelism Explosion is another good means of sharing the good news of Jesus. There are several

others. Share your testimony about how you came to Christ. Your "BC" experience which is your "Before Christ" living and lifestyle. Then your "AC" experience which is your "After Christ" came in your life.

**BE KIND.**

1 Peter 3:15 - but sanctify Christ as Lord in your hearts, always *being* **ready** to make a defense to everyone who asks you to give an account for the hope that is in you, yet with gentleness and reverence.

I cannot begin to say how important it is to be kind. Christians should be known for their kindness. Don't talk down to people. Don't be harsh or argue. Stay on message. There are several paths that you can get sidetracked on. Keep the conversation on Jesus and His saving grace.

# From Within

THERE IS AN INVADER WHO IS WITHIN. He consumes and destroys. He carries about his business often without being noticed. He doesn't work quickly, but he does work assuredly and consistently. Unnoticed by most.

In Honolulu, Hawaii sits a beautiful and historic building, the Iolani Palace. The palace was the royal residence of the kingdom of Hawaii. Unbeknown to anyone, as it stood strong and mighty, there was an enemy that was destroying the palace from the inside. It was a gradual, both sure destruction. And it went unnoticed. That is until the structure started showing signs of weakness.

The enemy? The Formosan termite.

Much has been written and said about the ultimate fall of the Roman Empire. There are many reasons for this fall. Perhaps as many as 8 are widely agreed upon. I will name 2 that are relevant to our talk today. These two were from within, decline in morals and values and political corruption.

Morality and values matter. Take these away and let each individual do as they please, and you will have chaos in a short time. Morality and values matter to God. When a society walks away or turns it back on a moral structure it will lose the favor and blessings of God.

Political corruption is too often commonplace. Bribery. Secret deals. Theft. Look at the annual salary of some public officials and ask yourself how is that they became wealthy through a career in political office?

The Roman Empire was slowly destroyed from within because of the dishonesty of its leaders.

Remember the termite. Although very small and seemingly insignificant, little by little, the palace was destroyed.

He hath shewed thee, O man, what is good; and what doth the Lord require of thee,

but to do justly, and to love mercy, and to walk humbly with thy God?

Micah 6:8

# Lead me to the Rock

My hope is built on nothing less
Than Jesus' blood and righteousness;
I dare not trust the sweetest frame,
But wholly lean on Jesus' name.
When darkness veils His lovely face,
I rest on His unchanging grace;
In every high and stormy gale,
My anchor holds within the veil.
On Christ, the solid Rock, I stand;
All other ground is sinking sand,
All other ground is sinking sand.

FROM THE END OF THE EARTH WILL I CRY unto thee, when my heart is overwhelmed: lead me to the rock that is higher than I.  Psalm 61:2

There is none holy as the Lord: for there is none beside thee: neither is there any rock like our God.  1 Samuel 2:2

The hymnal, the Hebrew hymnal (which we call the book of Psalms) and modern hymnals, are full of songs that reference the word "rock." Twenty six times the word "rock" is mentioned in the book of Psalms as speaking of the Lord.

Jesus referenced building our lives upon the rock in one of His teachings which is found in Matthew 7:24-27- the words of that teaching are:

Therefore whosoever hears these sayings of mine, and does them, I will liken him unto a wise man, which built his house upon a rock:

[25] And the rain descended, and the floods came, and the winds blew, and beat upon that house; and it fell not: for it was founded upon a rock.

[26] And every one that hears these sayings of mine, and does them not, shall be likened unto a foolish man, which built his house upon the sand:

[27] And the rain descended, and the floods came, and the winds blew, and beat upon that house; and it fell: and great was the fall of it.

*You build your life upon the Rock which is Jesus Christ and you will save your life from a multitude of problems that are avoidable.*
*Matthew 7:24-27*

# The Wounded Traveler

THIS STORY IS BASED UPON Luke 10:25-37

There is a man lying in a ditch; beaten half to death. A group of young men have beaten him, robbed him, and left him naked on this cold night. He is too weak to get out of the ditch. His hearing is intact and his mind is thinking so many thoughts at the same time. He believes he will die and he thinks about his life with thoughts of regret about the past. There is a certain fear in his heart. The thought "I am dying" comes to him. So, this is how it ends.

As he lies there, he hears a voice that is getting nearer to him. He tries to cry out, but is not able. He saw a man standing and looking down from the roadway. The man paused, looked at him, and kept walking.

People passing by. People passing by. He hears the conversations and laughter of a small group as it walks by. Some are too busy to notice. Some don't want to get involved.

He thinks, "maybe this is justice, I've never helped anyone."

He begins thinking about death, "so you don't go to death, death comes to you."

Then what?

He hears footsteps. Someone has stopped and is looking at him. The man speaks to him, but he is unable to answer him.

The man says, "That's all right. We'll get you some help and then find out who you are and where you belong."

He leaves for a moment, returns and begins cleaning his wounds. The man lifts the wounded stranger up and puts him on his donkey. He travels a short distance, stopping at an inn.

He hears him asking the innkeeper to look after him. He tells the innkeeper that when he returns, he will pay him for his care.

The man awakens and the innkeeper approaches him. He asked, "Who was that man who helped me? People walked by, a couple of them went to the other side of the road."

The innkeeper said, "He was just an ordinary man."

The "Good Samaritan" was an average man who helped someone in need. When you see someone in need, help them.

It is the Jesus way.

# Looking Forward

Brethren, I count not myself to have apprehended: but this one thing I do, forgetting those things which are behind, and reaching forth unto those things which are before - Philippians 3:13

I DON'T KNOW WHAT THE SIZE RATIO of the average windshield is to the rearview mirror? That would be one of those trivial facts in life that someone might know or have at least pondered?

I do know that for utilitarian and practical reasons that the windshield is much larger. It is manufactured in such a way that not only can you see through it, but you also have good visual angles.

Attached to the windshield is a rearview mirror. You don't look through it, but rather at it. It tells you where you have been, among other things.

My point here is that I think it's more important for us to see where we are going rather than where we have been. The past is the past is the past.

The Apostle Paul says in Philippians, chapter 3, that his practice was to forget the things that are behind...

The Bible does not "waste" its words. There is a reason that this verse is in the Bible. I think that I understand a little bit about why, too. It is the nature of humans oftentimes to dwell or ruminate on their past. I've heard on more than just a few occasions individuals relive and lament their past over and over. It's as if they are securely fastened or anchored to it and can't go forward.

Consider this, also - If you are driving and spend all of your time looking through the rearview mirror, you would almost certainly be a participant in a car wreck.

God says a great deal about past sins and lifestyles. The nation of Israel was often the starring cast of bad and wrong behavior. A couple of verses of Scripture come to mind about their past, and God's character:

Jeremiah 31:34...for I will forgive their iniquity, and I will remember their sin no more.

Malachi 7:18...He retains not His anger forever, because He delights in mercy.

Another thing worth pointing out is that the Apostle Paul stated, "this one thing I do." "This one thing" is about priority. This is so importance that it determines your future days and where you are going in your journey in life. We are not speaking of salvation, but victorious Christian living.

The argument and objection from you might be, "but I just can't do that." Yes, you can. But not in your own strength. It is the Lord who speaks this truth and by His strength that you will have victory. Declare your spiritual weakness to and before Him now. Cry out with the true voice of despair and defeat. You must go through the pain of Calvary to get to the victory of resurrection.

Our society says "be strong." Joyful is the one who perceives and learns that outside of the Lord's provision and indwelling Power that this is not possible. So, declare your weakness before Him.

Now, this forgetting is not a sweeping amnesia of the mind. It is in the looking forward toward Christ that we "forget." The past is no longer preeminent. It is no longer the first and/or lingering thought of our days. Your sins and your past has been forgiven by the Lord. So, don't keep digging up those "grave clothes" and wearing them.

Believe what God says about your sins – they are forgiven.

It's about looking forward (the windshield), not the past (the rear view mirror).

*And their sins and iniquities will I remember no more*
                                                        Hebrews 10:17.

# God Leads His Dear Children

God leads His dear children along; Where the water's cool flow bathes the weary one's feet,
God leads His dear children along.
Some through the waters, some through the flood,
Some through the fire, but all through the blood;
Some through great sorrow, but God gives a song,
In the night season and all the day long.
Sometimes on the mount where the sun shines so bright,
God leads His dear children along;
Sometimes in the valley, in darkest of night,
God leads His dear children along.

THIS SONG WAS WRITTEN BY GEORGE YOUNG, who was said to be a humble man who pastored small churches and worked as a carpenter. While away preaching, his home was burned and totally destroyed by some local hooligans. It was after this experience of losing everything that he penned this song.

*He leads me in paths of righteousness for his name's sake.*

Psalm 23:3

*The sheep hear his voice, and he calls his own sheep by name and leads them out.*

John 10:3

We should be known as those who follow and adore Jesus. No matter where life takes us. No matter what we must go through, we follow the Saviour.

And we follow Him regardless of life's challenges and trials.

Let us be true to our God.

www.ingramcontent.com/pod-product-compliance
Lightning Source LLC
Chambersburg PA
CBHW060854050426
42453CB00008B/978